Mommy, Where Do Butterflies Go?

by Leta Laugle

Illustrations by Erika Cooperman

CITI OF BOOKS

CITIOFBOOKS, INC.
3736 Eubank NE Suite A1
Albuquerque, NM 87111-3579
www.citiofbooks.com

Hotline: 1 (877) 389-2759
Fax: 1 (505) 930-7244

Ordering Information:
Quantity sales. Special discounts are available on quantity purchases by corporations, associations, and others. For details, contact the publisher at the address above.

Printed in the United States of America.

ISBN-13:	Softcover	978-1-960952-57-8
	Hardcover	978-1-960952-72-1
	eBook	978-1-960952-58-5

Library of Congress Control Number: 2023910890

DEDICATION

I would like to dedicate this book to my mother, Sally. I was visited by the rare, yellow swallowtail butterfly the day my mother passed and every day thereafter for many weeks. It brought me great comfort knowing she was there with me through my grief and my healing. I hope this book brings you similar comfort, as you are reminded, or realize, that we never truly lose those we love the most. This book is a dedication to all of those we love who have gone before us and those we cherish.

I like to take walks on a summer day to see the flowers bloom and watch the clouds float by. I particularly like to watch a small, fuzzy, caterpillar inch along on the ground.

I have watched a caterpillar build its amazing little cocoon house and hang upside down on a limb of a twig. After many days, the caterpillar decides to wake up, but it will no longer be a caterpillar, at least that is what Mommy and Daddy told me because God would show me a miracle very soon. So, I waited and watched.

Very soon, the most beautiful, big yellow butterfly came out of that tiny little cocoon. It took a very long time for the butterfly to spread her wings but once she did, she flapped and flapped until she took flight.

She slowly went from flower to flower, staying for a second or two it seemed to eat a little bit, then she came and rested on my finger, almost to say "Hello"! Oh, how I love butterflies! They are such happy creatures! I wonder where they go?

That same day when I arrived back home, my parents told me that my grandmother had gone to heaven. All that happy feeling I had with the butterfly in the garden had vanished and now I was so very sad.

I would not see my grandmother anymore. She was so special to me as we made cookies together, sang songs, and took long walks outside.

Mommy, Daddy, and I went to church for Grandma's "Celebration of her Life". It was a sad time.

Then a butterfly came to be with me which made me happy.

The next day a butterfly came to my window, again it made me smile!

The following day I saw another butterfly.

Finally, I ask "Mommy, where do the Butterflies go? Do Butterflies go to Heaven, too?" Mommy's reply, "God is all around us. He sends us comfort whenever we need it, like butterflies. All we have to do is trust, believe, and pray."

To My Illustrator, Erika Cooperman – Thank you so much for all of your hard work, professionalism, creativity, and most of all, beautiful artwork. Without you, this book would not have been completed. Thank you.

To My Loving Husband, Jeff – Thank you for all of your love and support. LUTT.

Printed in the USA
CPSIA information can be obtained
at www.ICGtesting.com
LVRC101142060124
768160LV00024B/1327

9 781960 952721